CHARLIE BROWN'S CYCLOPEDIA

A GUIDE TO PLANET EARTH

From the Ground Up

VOLUME · 7 ·

Based on the Charles M. Schulz Characters

Funk & Wagnalls

Charlie Brown's 'Cyclopedia has been produced by Mega-Books of New York, Inc. in conjunction with the editorial, design, and marketing staff of Field Publications.

STAFF FOR MEGA-BOOKS

Pat Fortunato
Editorial Director

Diana Papasergiou
Production Director

Susan Lurie
Executive Editor

Rosalind Noonan
Senior Editor

Adam Schmetterer
Research Director

Michaelis/Carpelis Design Assoc., Inc.
Art Direction and Design

STAFF FOR FIELD PUBLICATIONS

Cathryn Clark Girard
Assistant Vice President, Juvenile Publishing

Elizabeth Isele
Executive Editor

Kristina Jones
Executive Art Director

Leslie Erskine
Marketing Manager

Elizabeth Zuraw
Senior Editor

Michele Italiano-Perla
Group Art Director

Kathleen Hughes
Senior Art Director

Photograph and Illustration Credits:
Mike Andrews/Earth Scenes, 30; Craig Aurness/West Light, 53; Jim Brandenburg/West Light, 44; E.R. Degginger, 15, 30, 35, 40; Tom Owen Edmunds/Image Bank, 26; Walter Hodges/West Light, 45; Breck P. Kent/Earth Scenes, 15, 16, 48; Bryce Lee, 16, 26, 38, 43, 51, 52, 55, 56; Guy Motil/West Light, 28; Patti Murray/Earth Scenes, 56; Bill Ross/West Light, 58; Mary Ellen Senor, 13, 14, 19, 22, 25, 33, 35, 39, 41; Stouffer Enterprises/Earth Scenes, 52; Bob Waterman/West Light, 29; Doug Wechsler/Earth Scenes, 22; Roger Werth/West Light, 20.

ISBN: 0-8374-0052-X

Part of the material in this volume was previously published in *Charlie Brown's Second Super Book of Questions and Answers.*

Funk & Wagnalls, founded in 1876, is the publisher of *Funk & Wagnalls New Encyclopedia*, one of the most widely owned home and school reference sets, and many other adult and juvenile educational publications.

INTRODUCTION

Welcome to volume 7 of *Charlie Brown's 'Cyclopedia!* Have you ever wondered how the mountains were made, or what causes rainbows, or why leaves change color in the fall? Charlie Brown and the rest of the *Peanuts* gang are here to help you find the answers to these questions and many more about our planet Earth. Have fun!

CONTENTS

Hidden in the Earth's mountains, rocks, and ground are secrets to our planet's past. So get out your shovel and flashlight—it's time to go exploring. Let's discover the mysteries of our planet Earth!

THE EARTH UNDER YOUR FEET

THE EARTH'S PAST

How was the Earth born?

Many scientists believe that more than four billion years ago, the Earth was a great spinning ball of dust and gases. Over a long period of time, the bits of dust and the gases moved closer together. Finally, they shrank and joined to become solid rock. All the movement caused by the shrinking made the Earth heat up. In fact, it got so hot that the rock melted into a gluey liquid.

After millions of years, the outer layer of the Earth, called the crust, cooled off. Because it cooled, it hardened into rock again, in the same way that melted chocolate hardens when it cools in the refrigerator. The inside of the Earth however, did not cool. It has stayed hot until today because of the great pressure at the center of the Earth. Another reason it has stayed hot is that certain minerals in the Earth give off a lot of energy and heat. Such minerals are called radioactive (ray-dee-oh-AK-tiv).

What is the Earth made of?

The Earth is a great ball of rock. Beneath its grass, soil, and oceans lie thousands of miles of rock.

If you could dig a hole deep into the Earth, here's what you would find. At first, you would see hard rock, like the kind you see above ground. The rock would feel cool when you touched it. This rock is part of the crust of the Earth.

As you went deeper, the crust would become hotter and hotter. From about 5 to 20 miles into the Earth's rock, it would be hot enough to roast you alive! In fact, scientists think that the temperature may reach as high as 1,600 degrees Fahrenheit.

If you could keep digging in spite of this heat, you would be digging in the part of the Earth called the mantle. Most of the rock here would be hard, but some would be soft and gluey—like very thick molasses. The temperature would still be rising. The center, or core, of the Earth could be as hot as 9,000 degrees Fahrenheit! Most of this core is probably liquid rock.

No one has ever been able to dig far enough to see or feel what the Earth is like deep inside. However, scientists have machines that can gather information without ever going below the ground.

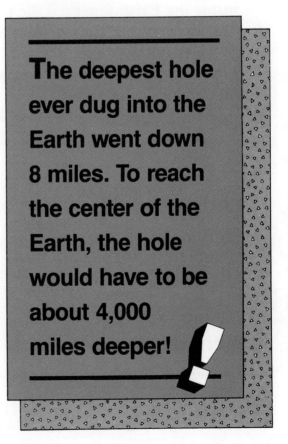

CRUST

MANTLE

INNER CORE

OUTER CORE

LAYERS OF THE EARTH

The deepest hole ever dug into the Earth went down 8 miles. To reach the center of the Earth, the hole would have to be about 4,000 miles deeper!

How were the mountains made?

Many mountains were made from rock that pushed up from the bottom of the ocean. Scientists know this because fossils of ancient sea animals are buried in the tops of the highest mountains. Fossils are the remains of plants and animals that have been buried in the Earth for many millions of years.

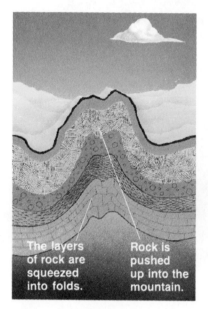

The layers of rock are squeezed into folds.

Rock is pushed up into the mountain.

Mud and sand, called sediment (SED-uh-ment), are always being carried by rivers from the land down into the oceans. Sediment that was carried to the oceans many millions of years ago came to rest in low places on the ocean floor. The skeletons of sea animals became mixed with the sediment. For hundreds of thousands of years, sediment piled up in layers on the ocean floor. The sand, mud, and skeletons got packed and squeezed together into solid rock. After many more thousands of years, forces inside the Earth squeezed the rock into folds—the way you can squeeze the skin on the back of your hand into folds. These forces pushed the folded rock upward to make many of the mountains we see today.

The continents of North America and Europe are moving apart about four centimeters each year— about as much as your fingernail grows!

ROCKS AND MINERALS

How many different kinds of rock are there?

There are three groups of rock. All rocks belong to one of the three groups.

The first group is called igneous (IG-nee-us) rock. This kind of rock started out as a hot liquid deep under the ground. Most igneous rock cooled and hardened underneath the Earth, but some of the liquid—lava—broke through to the Earth's surface. It flowed out from volcanoes and then hardened. One type of igneous rock, granite, is often used to make statues and buildings because it is very strong.

The second group of rock was made from sand, mud, clay, or animal and plant remains that rivers washed down from the land into the sea. It was packed down on the ocean floor in layers. Later, much of this rock rose again to make mountains. This kind of rock is called sedimentary (sed-uh-MEN-tuh-ree) rock. Cement is made from a sedimentary rock called limestone.

The third kind of rock is one that was once either igneous or sedimentary rock, but for millions of years it was bent, folded, twisted, squeezed, and heated by forces in the Earth. Because of this action, it was changed into a different kind of rock, called metamorphic (met-uh-MORE-fik) rock. The name means "rock that has been changed." The "lead" in a pencil is really graphite, which comes from a metamorphic rock.

TYPES OF ROCK

GRANITE—
Igneous

LIMESTONE—
Sedimentary

GRAPHITE—
Metamorphic

What are rocks made of?

All rocks are made of minerals. Minerals are found only in nature. They are never made by people. All of them are made of pieces called crystals. There are thousands of known minerals in the world. They have different colors, feel different to the touch, and have different strengths. If you look closely at most rocks, you will see speckles in them. These speckles are minerals.

How soft can a mineral be?

A mineral can be soft enough to be scratched with your fingernail. This means that your fingernail is harder than the mineral. Talc is one of these very soft minerals. It is so soft, in fact, that baby powder is made from it! Most minerals, however, are harder.

What is the hardest mineral?

A diamond is the hardest of all minerals. The only thing that can scratch a diamond is another diamond. Because diamonds are so rare and hard and beautiful, they are very valuable and are used to make rings and other jewelry.

This is how a diamond looks when it is mined.

16

SOIL

What is soil?

Soil is the dark brown covering over most land. It can be a few inches or a few feet thick. Some people call soil "dirt."

Soil is made mostly of tiny bits of rock. Soil also contains water, air, and pieces of plants and animals that have died. Mixed in with soil, too, are small living things such as bacteria (back-TEER-ee-uh). These living things are so tiny you need a microscope to see them.

How was soil formed?

Billions of years ago, when the Earth was young, there was no soil. Only water and rock lay on the surface of the Earth. Then rain, wind, swift rivers, and ocean waves began to pound at the rocks. Slowly, they wore the rock down, and water seeped into cracks in the rock. In cold weather, the water froze. Frozen water—ice—takes up more space than liquid water. The ice pushed against both sides of a crack and split the rock into stones. Rain and rivers washed the stones down rocky mountains, wearing them down into smaller rocks and pebbles. After millions of years, a layer of very tiny pieces of rock built up on the surface of the Earth. Pieces of dead plants and animals got mixed in with the bits of rock. This mixture is soil.

CHAPTER 2

THE EARTH IN MOTION

Although the Earth may seem quiet and still, it's full of amazing power. There are exploding volcanoes that look like the biggest Fourth of July fireworks show you could ever imagine. There are earthquakes that sometimes have the strength of a thousand bulldozers. Let's look at the many different ways the Earth is in action.

FIERY VOLCANOES

Does hot rock ever come out of the Earth?

Yes. Hot, liquid rock, called lava, comes out of volcanoes. Scientists give the name *volcano* to any crack in the Earth's crust from which lava flows. Lava can be up to ten times hotter than boiling water.

Scientists are not sure why a volcano becomes active, or erupts. They think that hot gases inside the Earth push lava up from below. The force of these gases may also cause the loud noise that a volcano makes when it erupts.

The Earth may shake when a volcano erupts. Fiery-hot, glowing lava, as well as steam, ashes, and even solid rocks shoot into the air. Once the lava reaches the surface of the Earth, it slowly cools and hardens. Often so much lava, rock, and ash come out that a mountain builds up around the crack. Then the whole mountain, with its crack, is called a volcano. Some volcanic mountains can take as long as ten thousand years to build up. Some have grown several hundred feet in a single day.

No volcano keeps erupting all the time. The rest period of a volcano varies from just a few minutes to several hundred years. Volcanoes that rest over many years are called dormant. When a volcano stops erupting altogether, we say it is extinct.

When the Earth heats up, hot lava and ash shoot from some volcanoes.

Are volcanoes dangerous?

Yes. The hot lava that pours out of a volcano often causes fires and can even bury a whole city. When a volcano erupts, it often sends out a cloud of poisonous gases that can kill or injure people who breathe the gases.

A Hawaiian volcano once threw out a block of stone that weighed as much as four big trucks. The stone landed half a mile away!

WHEN THE EARTH SHAKES

What is an earthquake?

Any snapping, breaking, or shifting of the Earth's crust is called an earthquake. The snapping makes the Earth shake, or quake.

Forces inside the Earth are always squeezing and straining the rock of the Earth's crust. Usually, these forces bend the rock but don't snap it, so there is no earthquake. Sometimes, however, the forces are so great that they make the rock snap. If you are close to where the rock has snapped, you feel the Earth shiver—you feel the earthquake.

Can an earthquake change the Earth's surface?

Yes. Big earthquakes can break off parts of mountains, tear open the ground, and shove huge chunks of land around. They can make buildings fall down and gas pipes burst, starting fires. Water pipes can break, so that there is no water to put out the fires. People can be killed by the falling buildings or the fire, but most earthquakes are small and do very little damage. In addition, many modern buildings are specially built to survive the shaking of an earthquake. If an earthquake does begin, don't panic. If you are inside, stand in a doorway, since doorways are strong. If you are outdoors, move away from buildings that could topple over.

Seismograph tapes show the Earth's movement.

Scientists use seismographs to measure the force of an earthquake.

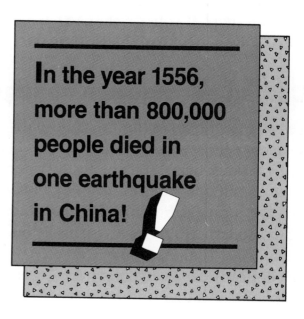

In the year 1556, more than 800,000 people died in one earthquake in China!

How do scientists measure the force of an earthquake?

Scientists have machines that measure movements in the Earth. These machines are called seismographs (SIZE-moe-graffs). The power of a quake is measured on the Richter (RIK-ter) scale. The scale starts at one. Each whole number higher means a ten-times increase in the power of the earthquake. For instance, an earthquake that measures five on the Richter scale is 10 times stronger than an earthquake that measures four, and 100 times stronger than one that measures three. An earthquake measuring two is very small and may not even be noticed. One measuring four and a half will cause some damage. An earthquake measuring six is very dangerous.

CHAPTER 3

Isn't water magical! Hold it in your hand, and it will flow out between your fingers. Put it in the freezer, and it becomes a solid block of ice! Water is a wonderful, wet, and wild part of our world.

WET AND WILD

OCEANS AND RIVERS

How many oceans are there in the world?

Even though we talk about the Atlantic Ocean, the Pacific Ocean and other oceans, there is really just one ocean. That's because each ocean is joined to the water of another ocean. The ocean has no end. You can see this if you make a small paper boat, and try sailing it around a globe. Start the boat at any point in the ocean, and keep it going in the water. Can you find a place where your boat must stop sailing? No.

How was the ocean formed?

The Earth did not always have a great ocean, as it does today. Many millions of years ago, the Earth was very hot. Some scientists believe that at that time, most of the Earth's water was trapped inside its rocks. Over a period of millions of years, the rocks began to cool and harden. As they got hard, their

IT'S ONE CONTINUOUS OCEAN!

water came out. It ran into the low places in the Earth's crust and made the first oceans.

Other scientists think the water came from clouds that were around the Earth. As the hot Earth cooled, the clouds cooled, too. Clouds that cool form raindrops, so the clouds around the Earth rained for hundreds of years, filling the Earth's low places.

Since then, the numbers, shapes, and sizes of the oceans have changed, but oceans are still large, low areas filled with water.

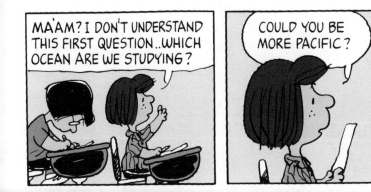

MA'AM? I DON'T UNDERSTAND THIS FIRST QUESTION..WHICH OCEAN ARE WE STUDYING?

COULD YOU BE MORE PACIFIC?

9-7

SPECIFIC. **WHATEVER.**

Where is the deepest part of the ocean?

The deepest spot is the Mariana Sea Trench in the Pacific Ocean. Here the water is more than 35,820 feet deep—or nearly seven miles from the surface to the bottom. That's deep enough to swallow the highest mountain in the world—Mount Everest—which is nearly six miles high.

If you were to drop a rock the size of your head into water 36,000 feet deep, it would take the rock about an hour to reach the bottom!

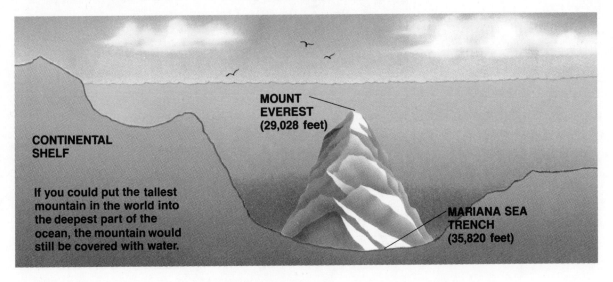

MOUNT EVEREST (29,028 feet)

CONTINENTAL SHELF

If you could put the tallest mountain in the world into the deepest part of the ocean, the mountain would still be covered with water.

MARIANA SEA TRENCH (35,820 feet)

25

NILE RIVER

Where do rivers come from?

Rivers start with rain. Wherever rain falls or snow melts, some water flows downhill. Water moves down toward the lowest place, carving out ditches in the ground. With every new rainfall, the water makes the ditches deeper and wider, forming streams that flow into other streams. They grow bigger and bigger until they become rivers. Rivers keep flowing along until they pour into the ocean.

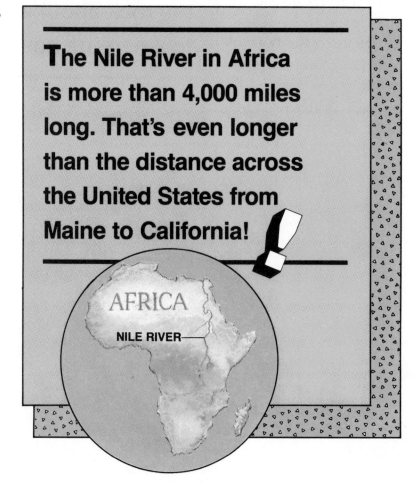

The Nile River in Africa is more than 4,000 miles long. That's even longer than the distance across the United States from Maine to California!

AFRICA

NILE RIVER

26

TIDES AND WAVES

What are tides?

Have you ever sat on a sandy beach and watched the ocean water move closer and closer to you? If you have, you were watching the tide come in. If you were still on the beach later that day, you saw the tide go out again. That means that the ocean water moved back. Once again, you could see the sand that the water had covered earlier in the day.

In most parts of the world, tides go in and out this way twice each day. They do so because the ocean water rises and falls. This rise and fall is caused by gravity—the great invisible force that all stars, planets, and moons have. The force of gravity pulls things. The gravity of the Sun and the gravity of the Moon both pull on the Earth's ocean water, causing tides. The Moon is much nearer the Earth than the Sun, so the Moon's pull on the ocean water is the stronger one. The Moon also pulls on the Earth's land, but the land is solid, so it doesn't move. Ocean water is liquid, so it moves more easily. Lakes and rivers have tides, too, but they are usually too small to be noticed.

People surf on waves like these on the coast of California.

LOOK WHAT THE SURF BROUGHT IN!

What makes the waves in the ocean?

Waves are ridges, or swells, of water on top of the ocean. They travel one after another across the ocean. Most waves are caused by wind blowing over the top of the water. When wind begins to blow over a smooth stretch of water, little ripples are formed. If the wind keeps blowing in the same direction, the ripples grow bigger. They get to be waves. The longer and harder the wind blows, the bigger the waves get.

What is a tidal wave?

A tidal wave has nothing to do with tides. It is a gigantic wave caused by an earthquake under the ocean. The quake pushes a part of the seafloor up or down and starts a long wave. The wave travels fast, sometimes hundreds of miles an hour. As it travels, it grows. At first, a tidal wave may be only a few feet high. By the time it reaches land, however, the tidal wave can grow to be 100 feet high. When it hits the shore, it can cause great damage. Today most scientists call a tidal wave by its Japanese name, *tsunami* (tsoo-NAH-mee).

28

FROZEN WATER

What is a glacier?

A glacier (GLAY-shur) is a huge heap of ice and snow so heavy that its own weight moves it downhill. Sometimes glaciers are called "rivers of ice." Like rivers, they keep moving downhill until they reach the ocean—unless they melt first. Glaciers move very slowly. Small ones may move only an inch or so a day. Large glaciers may move as much as ten feet a day.

Where do glaciers come from?

In some parts of the world, a lot of snow falls. If the temperature doesn't warm up, new snow piles up on top of old snow. As years go by, the growing heap of snow gets thicker and heavier. Gradually, most of it gets packed down into ice. When the heap gets very, very heavy, it begins to slide downhill. It has become a moving glacier.

As this ship moves through the water, passengers can look up at the beautiful glaciers of Alaska.

An iceberg in Baffin Bay, which separates Canada and Greenland.

What is an iceberg?

An iceberg is a mountain of ice floating in the ocean. It was once part of a glacier, but it broke off when the glacier reached the edge of the ocean.

Although an iceberg is born in a very cold place, when it floats out to a warmer area it begins to melt. The iceberg travels and melts little by little. Eventually, it gets very soft, breaks into pieces, and melts away completely. Whatever its size, most of an iceberg's ice is hidden below the surface of the water. What people see is just the tip of the ice sticking out above the water.

Some icebergs are thousands of times larger than a football field. The largest, sighted in 1956 off the coast of Antarctica, was 208 miles long and 60 miles wide!

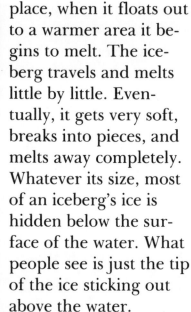

NO, THERE AREN'T ANY ICEBERGS IN THE BIRDBATH.

CHAPTER 4

No matter where you go or what you do, weather affects your life each and every day. When summer comes and the weather is sunny and warm, you can go outside and play without a coat! When winter arrives and the cold winds blow, it's time to bundle up from head to toe. What makes weather change? The *Peanuts* gang is here to tell you.

HOW'S THE WEATHER?

WEATHER AND CLIMATE

What is weather?

When you talk about weather, you are really talking about the air. How hot or cold is the air? How much dampness, or moisture, is in it? How fast is the air moving? How heavily does it press on the Earth? The answers to these questions tell about the weather.

IT'S HOT TODAY...

I WISH WE HAD A POOL OR LIVED NEAR A LAKE..

WELL, THERE'S ONLY ONE THING TO DO...

GO DOWN TO THE OL' SWIMMING BUCKET!

© 1985 United Feature Syndi...

What's the difference between weather and climate?

Weather tells what the air is like in a place at any one time. Climate tells what the weather is like in general, all year round. If a place has much more dry weather than wet weather, we say it has a dry climate. If it has much more hot weather than cold weather, we say it has a hot climate. Tucson, Arizona, for example, has a hot, dry climate. On most summer, spring, and fall days in Tucson, the weather is dry, sunny, and hot. Though the temperature cools a bit in winter, Tucson's climate is still mostly sunny, dry, and hot.

Weather changes each day. Climate stays much the same one year after another, but it may change over periods of hundreds or thousands of years.

What makes climates different?

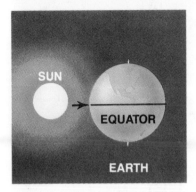

The location of a place on the Earth decides its climate. If you live close to either the North Pole or the South Pole, you live in a cold climate. The Sun's rays hit these areas at a great slant and don't warm the land very much. But if you live somewhere around the middle of the Earth—near what we call the equator (ih-KWAY-tur)—your hometown probably has a climate that is hot all year round. That is because the Sun's rays hit this area fairly directly. The more directly the Sun's rays hit a place, the warmer that place is. If you live near the equator, your hometown not only gets more Sun, but it also gets more rain than places very far north or south.

How high up you live also makes a difference in the climate. In the mountains, you are likely to have a cooler climate than at a lower level.

If you live near the ocean, your winters are warmer and your summers cooler than those in places far from the ocean. Your town usually has more rain than inland places, too. Winds and the movement of water in the ocean near your home also help to make your climate the way it is.

IT'S NEVER TOO HOT FOR JOE COOL.

FORECASTING THE WEATHER

How do weather forecasters know what tomorrow's weather will be?

Tomorrow's weather is already forming in the air above the Earth. Weather forecasters get reports from many thousands of weather stations on what is happening to the air all around the world. These stations measure the temperature and the amount of rain or snow that falls. They also measure how much moisture the air holds, and how fast the weather is carried by planetary (PLAN-ih-tair-ee) winds—winds that blow all the time over large areas of the Earth. Airlines and ships at sea send radio messages every few hours about the weather where they are. Cameras and other kinds of equipment circle the Earth in weather satellites, sending back pictures and other information. All these facts are put together on special maps that show what kind of weather is heading your way.

AH! ACCORDING TO THE WEATHER FORECAST, I'LL HAVE CLEAR SKIES ALL WEEK.

What do forecasters mean when they say the barometer is rising?

In a weather report, the weather forecaster may say that the barometer (buh-ROM-uh-tur) is rising or falling. A barometer is a special instrument that measures how heavily the air is pressing on the Earth. When the barometer is rising, it means that the air is pressing harder on the Earth.

When the barometer is falling, it means the air is pressing less on the Earth.

Knowing the air pressure helps people predict the weather. When the air pressure is rising, clear skies and cool weather are probably on their way. When the air pressure is falling, stormy weather is probably in store for us.

The word *high* circled on a weather map shows the center of high air pressure. The word *low* shows the center of low air pressure.

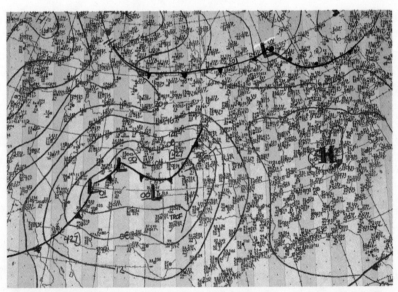

This is a picture of a weather map. Forecasters use maps such as this to tell us whether we'll have rain or sunny skies.

What do forecasters mean by humidity?

Humidity is the moisture, or water vapor, in the air. If there is a lot of water vapor in the air, the humidity is high. If there is very little water vapor in the air, the humidity is low.

What are cold fronts and warm fronts?

A large mass of air with about the same amount of moisture and temperature is called a front. A cold front is the leading edge of a cold air mass. It often brings showers and thunderstorms with fast winds. A warm front is the leading edge of a warm air mass. If often brings steady rains or snow.

35

CLOUDS, FOG, DEW, AND FROST

What makes a cloud?

A cloud is made up of very tiny drops of water, called cloud droplets. Air always has some water vapor in it. If the air is warm, it is light, and it rises. As it rises, it cools. Cool air cannot hold as much water vapor as warm air, so the particles of water vapor join together, or condense. They usually condense around tiny specks of dust or salt in the air and form water droplets. If the air is very cold, they form bits of ice called ice crystals. The water droplets and ice crystals are light enough to float in the air. Any one droplet or ice crystal is too small for the eye to see, but a whole crowd of them makes a cloud.

The big fluffy clouds that you see in the sky are called cumulonimbus clouds.

What is fog?

A cloud that forms close to the ground is called fog. If you walk in fog, you cannot see separate little droplets, but you can often feel them on your face. A whole crowd of droplets can make such a thick fog cloud that you cannot see through it.

SO, WHAT'S THE HOLD UP? WHY AREN'T WE MOVING?

What is smog?

The word *smog* is a combination of the words *smoke* and *fog*—and that's pretty much what smog is. The air always has some bits of dust floating around in it. In cities, the air also contains other particles— soot and smoke from chimneys, chemicals from factories, and fumes from automobile exhaust. We say such air is polluted. On breezy days, moving air carries the polluting particles away. On still days, a blanket of air heavy with moisture may hang over the city. Then none of the dirty particles blow away. Water droplets form around them. The dark cloud or fog they make is called smog. When you breathe in a lot of the dirty particles all at once, your lungs can be hurt. Smog is the worst kind of air pollution.

SORRY, CHUCK! I JUST COULDN'T SEE YOU IN ALL THIS FOG.

Where does dew come from?

Dew is moisture from the air that has gathered in drops on leaves and blades of grass. At night the Earth and the air near it usually cool off. So do grasses and other plants. Cool air cannot hold as much moisture as warm air can, so some of the moisture in the air condenses into drops of water on the leaves and grass. These drops are dew.

1. Heat from the Sun causes moisture from the Earth to evaporate into the warm air.

2. After sunset, the air and the Earth cool. Moisture condenses, and dewdrops form.

What is frost?

Frost is like dew. When the night is very cold, however, the moisture in the air forms ice, or frost, instead of water, or dew. Like dew, frost forms on grasses and other plants.

IT'S WINDY OUTSIDE!

What makes the winds blow?

The air around us is always moving. It moves because the air pressure is different in different places. When air is warmed by the sun, it gets lighter. It rises and then moves to a spot with colder air. The colder air sinks and then moves to the warm area. You feel this movement as wind.

There are two kinds of wind. One kind blows within a small area. For example, the air in a cloudy place is cooler than the air in a sunny place. The temperature difference causes the air to move, or the wind to blow.

The planetary winds are the second kind of wind. They blow all the time over large areas of the Earth. They move between cool parts of the Earth near the North Pole and South Pole and warm parts of the Earth near the equator. Planetary winds move clouds and storms from one place to another.

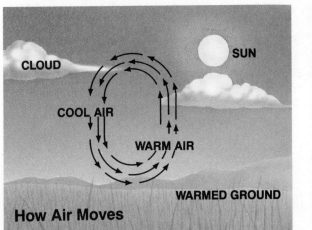

How Air Moves

How fast is the wind?

Near the ground, winds usually blow more slowly than a car moves on a highway—less than 50 miles an hour. High up in the air, winds blow faster. Wind gusts of up to 231 miles an hour have been measured at the top of Mount Washington, in New Hampshire. That is about as fast as a race car in the Indy 500!

39

TORNADOES AND HURRICANES

The funnel of this tornado looks black because of all the dust it's sweeping along.

What is a tornado?

A tornado is a noisy, funnel-shaped windstorm that often sweeps across parts of the United States and western Africa. It looks like a long sleeve reaching down from a huge dark cloud. In a tornado, wind whirls around and around in a circle about the size of two or three football fields. Very little air is in the center of this circle. Like a giant vacuum cleaner, the tornado can suck up anything in its path. Up go houses, cars, animals, people, and even railroad tracks. They may come down again later, far from where the storm picked them up. That's what happened to Dorothy and her dog, Toto, in *The Wizard of Oz*. A tornado can also flatten big buildings or even make them explode.

The whirling winds of a tornado can spin as fast as 280 miles an hour, but the whole tornado, spinning like a top, moves along at 20 to 40 miles an hour—about the speed of a car traveling down a city street.

What is a hurricane?

A hurricane is a wild windstorm that starts at sea. Like a tornado, a hurricane is made up of whirling winds. Unlike a tornado, a hurricane is very large. It usually stretches across 300 or 400 miles at one time.

Inside a hurricane, the wind is whirling at speeds of from 75 to 200 miles an hour. A hurricane's wild winds cause huge waves to form on the ocean. The waves can sink ships, and the wind can tear up trees and buildings along the coast. Hurricanes usually bring heavy rains, too. These rains, as well as the high waves, can cause floods.

Eye of the storm

All of this area is getting the storm

HURRICANE OVER FLORIDA

What is the eye of the storm?

At the center of a hurricane's circle of whirling winds is a quiet space with clear skies above. This is the "eye" of a hurricane. It is usually about 20 miles across. Some people think the hurricane is over when the eye of the storm reaches them. The wind dies down, and the sky is bright above, but the whole storm circle is still traveling. In a few hours, the other side of the whirlwind will arrive, bringing more wild winds and heavy rains.

How are hurricanes named?

In the early 1900s, an Australian weatherman, Clement Wragge, began naming hurricanes after people he didn't like, particularly politicians. Now male and female names are chosen years in advance for naming future hurricanes.

I WONDER IF THERE'S EVER BEEN A "HURRICANE LUCY"?

CHAPTER 5

The wind is blowing, the sky is gray, and the rain won't go away—but don't worry! It's a perfect day to stay inside with Charlie Brown and the gang. They're here to tell you more about storms, from rainstorms to hailstorms to fluffy white snowstorms.

STORMY WEATHER

RAIN

Where does rain come from?

Rain comes from clouds. When a cloud grows big, the cloud droplets in it begin to bump into one another. They join together and form big drops. The big drops are too heavy to float in the air, so they fall to Earth as rain.

Raindrops are not tear-shaped as artists often draw them. They are perfectly round!

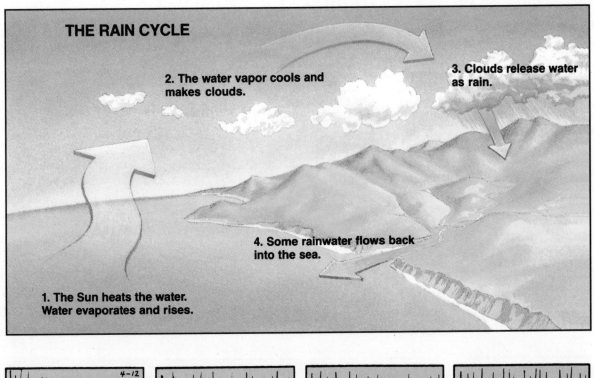

THE RAIN CYCLE

2. The water vapor cools and makes clouds.

3. Clouds release water as rain.

4. Some rainwater flows back into the sea.

1. The Sun heats the water. Water evaporates and rises.

Why are deserts so dry?

Deserts are dry because they get very little rain. Many deserts are separated from the sea by mountains. Winds that blow onto the land from the sea carry a lot of moisture. When the winds start blowing up mountain slopes, they become cooler. Cooler winds cannot hold as much moisture as warmer ones. So the cooled-off winds drop their moisture in the form of rain or snow before reaching the mountaintops. By the time the winds reach the other side of the mountains, almost no moisture is left in them. The land on the other side of the mountains gets very little rain. It can become a desert.

AN AFRICAN DESERT

The Atacama Desert in Chile has been almost rainless for more than 400 years!

Which place on Earth gets the most rain?

A spot on the Hawaiian island of Kauai (kah-oo-AH-ee) gets about 460 inches of rain each year. That's at least 400 inches more than most other places in the United States.

THUNDER AND LIGHTNING

What causes thunderstorms?

We have thunderstorms when big, fluffy-looking clouds, called thunder-heads, tower very high into the sky. They look beautiful when you see them at a distance. When the sun shines on their high-piled puffs, they look white, but as they sweep overhead and shut out the sunlight, they look very dark.

These clouds build up on hot, damp days when the very warm ground heats the moist air above it. The air rises higher and faster than usual. Water drop-lets gather into very big clouds. Some are several miles high! Inside each cloud, the warm, rising air cools quickly and sinks to a lower part of the cloud. There, the air is warmed again, and it rises. This rising and falling air makes violent winds inside the cloud. Large raindrops form, lightning flashes, and thunder crashes.

After a lightning bolt this size, loud thunder is sure to follow.

What is lightning?

Lightning is a flash of electricity in the air. There is electricity everywhere—in clouds, in the Earth, even in you! Sometimes when you walk across a carpet and touch someone, you feel a tiny spark of electricity jump between the two of you.

In towering thunderclouds, a lot of electricity builds up. As clouds draw near one another, huge flashes of electricity pass between two clouds, or from a cloud to Earth. The electricity heats the air along the path of the flash so much that the air glows. That glow is what we call lightning.

45

Each second of every day, about 100 bolts of lightning strike some part of the Earth!

What is thunder?

When air is heated, the very tiny particles that make it up begin to move faster. The electrical flash from a thundercloud suddenly heats the air so much that all the particles move around wildly. The air shakes, as huge numbers of them suddenly rush apart. When this sudden huge movement in the air reaches our ears, we hear a thunderclap.

Why do you see the lightning before you hear the thunder?

Light travels fast—186,282 miles in one second! So you see the glow of lightning the instant it flashes, even though it may be miles away. Sound travels much more slowly. It takes the sound of thunder nearly five seconds to travel one mile. So if a lightning flash is one mile away, you see the light right away. Then the sky darkens again, and after about five seconds, you hear the thunder.

ARGH!

Can thunder and lightning hurt you?

Thunder can't hurt you, but lightning can. Thunder is just air shaking very hard. Lightning is electricity. A very small flash of electricity can give you a shock. A lightning flash is huge. It can burn whatever it touches, sometimes very badly.

Lightning usually strikes the highest thing around. This may be a skyscraper in a city, a tall tree in an open field, or a sailboat mast on the water. Metal lightning rods or specially wired television antennas can lead the electricity safely to the ground. They can keep a building safe from lightning damage. A metal car or airplane body can protect people inside it, too. However, if you stand under a big tree, you will not be protected. The tree may be hit by lightning, and so may you. So if you are outside during a thunderstorm, you will be safest lying flat on the ground!

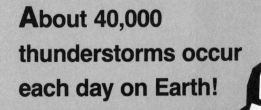

About 40,000 thunderstorms occur each day on Earth!

47

FREEZING RAIN AND SNOW

What is hail?

Hail is made up of small lumps of ice that sometimes fall to Earth during thunderstorms. These icy stones are formed inside the thunderclouds. The tops of tall thunderheads are always very cold. Down near the bottoms of the

Hailstones come in many shapes and sizes.

clouds, the air is much warmer. Inside these clouds, warm air moves swiftly up, and cold air moves swiftly down. Sometimes raindrops are blown up to the freezing-cold part of the cloud before they fall. There they turn to ice. Then they are blown down again and are coated with more raindrops. Before they fall to Earth, the bits of ice may be blown up and down many times. Each time, more raindrops gather on them and then freeze, forming extra layers of ice on the lump. Each lump of ice is called a hailstone.

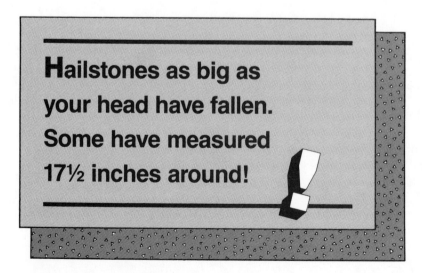

Hailstones as big as your head have fallen. Some have measured 17½ inches around!

What is sleet?

Sleet is frozen rain. It falls when the air close to the ground is freezing cold. Sleet starts out as rain. As the raindrops fall, they freeze. They form the tiny ice balls known as sleet.

48

Is snow frozen rain?

No. Raindrops that freeze as they fall form sleet, not snow. Snowflakes are formed right in the clouds. Clouds floating in freezing-cold air are made up of tiny crystals of ice. As the air grows colder, more and more water vapor condenses around the ice. The tiny crystals grow bigger and bigger. The snowflakes you see are simply these crystals after they have grown too large and heavy to float in the air. They fall to Earth as snow.

What do snowflakes look like?

If you look closely at a group of snowflakes, you will see that they are like small, lacy crystals. Snowflakes have many different sizes, shapes, and lovely patterns. However, if you count their sides, you will find that each snowflake has six sides, and each has six points, too.

No two snow-flakes are exactly alike!

CHAPTER 6

Planet Earth wouldn't be the same without green fields of clover, giant redwood trees, and colorful flowers. You'll find some plants on your dinner table as vegetables. Plants also perform a special task that gives us air to breathe! Let's take a look at the amazing plants in our world.

THE EARTH IN BLOOM!

ALL ABOUT PLANTS

What is a plant?

Anything that is alive and isn't an animal is a plant. Unlike animals, most plants stay in one place. They don't walk, swim, or fly. Most plants have green leaves, which contain the chemical compound chlorophyll (KLAWR-uh-fill). Chlorophyll gives leaves their green color. Some plants with chlorophyll don't have green leaves. They have red, purple, or brown leaves instead.

How many kinds of plants are there?

There are more than 360,000 different kinds of plants on the Earth. They come in all sizes. Some are so tiny that you can see them only under a microscope. Others are so large that they tower hundreds of feet above the ground. In fact, the tallest living thing, the giant redwood tree, is a plant.

Plants have many different shapes, too. A blade of grass is long and skinny. Palm trees have large leaves and long trunks. Cabbages are round and leafy. A cactus is narrow with sharp spines. Mushrooms are umbrella-shaped, and lichens (LIKE-inz) spread out like a carpet.

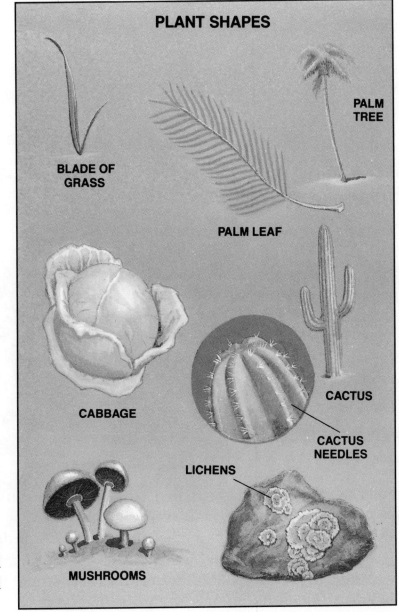

PLANT SHAPES

BLADE OF GRASS

PALM LEAF

PALM TREE

CABBAGE

CACTUS

CACTUS NEEDLES

LICHENS

MUSHROOMS

How can you tell how old a tree is?

When a tree is cut down, you can usually see rings in the tree stump. The rings show how many years the tree was growing.

Each spring, a tree grows new wood. This light-colored wood grows around the old, dark wood of the tree trunk. So if you count the number of dark-colored rings, you will know how many years the tree lived.

Each ring in a tree shows one year's growth.

How long have plants been on the Earth?

Plants have been on the Earth for more than 400 million years. The first plants were tiny water plants, the kind you can see only under a microscope. They were on the Earth about 200 million years before the dinosaurs. In fact, they were here long before any animals.

Some bristlecone pine trees have lived nearly 5,000 years!

What would happen if all the plants on the Earth died?

If all the plants on the Earth died, so would all the animals, including people. We need plants in order to live. When plants make food, they give off oxygen (OCK-suh-jin), a gas that animals must breathe in order to stay alive.

Animals also depend on plants for their food. All animals eat either plants or plant-eating animals. Without plants, there would be almost no food on the Earth! All of the animals on Earth would die.

SEEDS

What's inside a seed?

The inside of every seed has a soft part called an embryo (EM-bree-oh). A new plant starts from the embryo and the soft food stored around it.

To make seeds, most flowers need pollen from another flower. When pollen from one flower gets on another, the plant is pollinated (POLL-in-ate-ed). Bees and wind help pollinate flowers.

SEED

SHELL

EMBRYO

How does a seed become a new plant?

The embryo forms while the seed is still on the plant. Once it is formed, it stops growing for a while. It will grow—germinate (GER-min-ate)—as soon as it is in the right soil with the right temperature and the right amount of water. Then the embryo will sprout roots and stems. It will grow leaves and start making its own food. The embryo will become a whole plant and make seeds of its own.

The feathery seeds of this flower are carried by the wind.

Do all new plants come from seeds?

Plants that have flowers come from seeds. Other plants start in other ways. Some plants send out long horizontal stems above the ground, called runners, to start new plants. Strawberries start plants this way. The leaf of some plants, such as the African violet, can be put into the ground, and new plants will grow from it. Other plants grow plantlets. These are whole plants that are smaller than the parent, but otherwise just like it. The plantlet stays attached to the parent until it grows to nearly full size. Then it splits off from the parent plant and lives on its own. Other plants grow tiny specks, called spores, instead of seeds. Each spore can produce a new plant. Look under the umbrella of a mushroom or on the underside of a fern leaf to see spores.

How are seeds spread so that plants grow in many different places?

The wind spreads seeds that are tiny or fluffy and can easily float in the air. It also spreads seeds that have "wings," such as maple seeds.

Water sometimes spreads these winged seeds, too. Any seeds that are able to float can be spread by water. Such seeds may travel long distances before they reach land again.

Animals also spread seeds. Some seeds have sharp hooks that get stuck to an animal's fur and fall off later. Burrs, or "stickers," are seeds of this kind. Some birds and other animals eat the fruits of trees. They may carry off the fruits and then drop the seeds far away.

LEAVES

Why do plants need leaves, roots, flowers, and stems?

Most plants make their own food. They use their leaves to make it.

Roots are needed to hold a plant firmly in the ground. The roots also take water and minerals out of the soil. The plant needs these things to live. Sometimes roots store some of the food that the leaves make.

Flowers are the parts of the plant where seeds can form. The seeds will someday be new plants.

Stems hold up the leaves and flowers to sunlight. Stems have tubes in them that carry liquids, called sap, up and down the plant. Some of the tubes bring water mixed with minerals from the roots to the leaves. Other tubes carry liquid food away from the leaves to the rest of the plant.

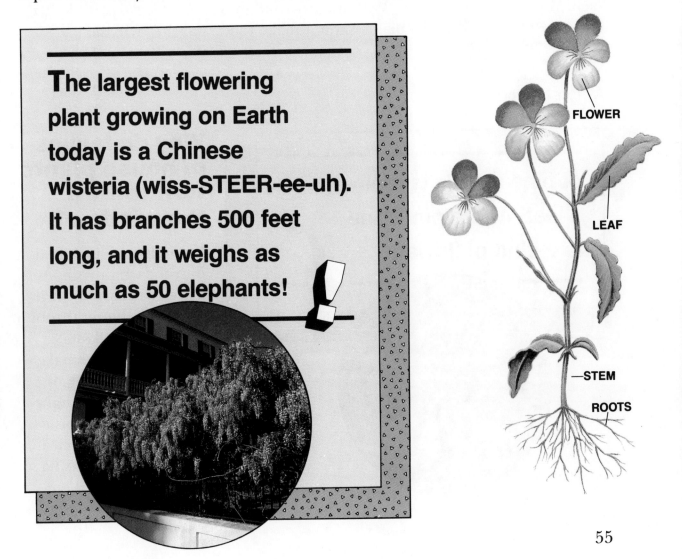

The largest flowering plant growing on Earth today is a Chinese wisteria (wiss-STEER-ee-uh). It has branches 500 feet long, and it weighs as much as 50 elephants!

FLOWER

LEAF

—STEM

ROOTS

How do leaves make food?

A "food factory"

The leaves of a plant are like little food factories. Inside them is the chemical chlorophyll that the leaves need to make food. The food factory needs sun to start working. When the Sun shines on the chlorophyll, each leaf factory goes to work.

The leaf factory uses two things to make food. It uses water that has come up from the soil through the roots and stems. It also uses a gas called carbon dioxide (die-OCK-side) that has come from the air through tiny openings in the leaf. From the water and carbon dioxide it makes sugar, which is the plant's food. At the same time, the factory makes a gas called oxygen. The plant sends this oxygen into the air.

Without any sunlight (or an electric plant light), plants cannot make food, and they will die.

A pine needle is really a leaf! And a pinecone is a kind of flower.

Why do leaves of house plants turn toward the window?

If you let a plant stand on your windowsill, its leaves will turn toward the light coming through the window. Plants need the light to make food. This turning of plants toward the light is called phototropism (foe-toe-TRO-piz-em).

Outdoors, plants have light all around them, so their leaves don't turn.

Why do leaves change color in the fall?

Leaves have many colors in them—green, red, orange, and yellow—but during the spring and summer, there is much more green than any other color. The green comes from the chlorophyll. The leaves have so much chlorophyll that it hides the other colors and you can't see them. In the fall, however, before cold weather sets in, many leaves stop making food. When they stop making food, the chlorophyll breaks down. As it breaks down, the colors that were hidden start to appear, and you can see them in the leaves.

Why do leaves drop off the trees in the fall?

During warm weather, the leaves of a tree are always giving off tiny drops of water. At the same time, the tree's roots are taking in more water so that the tree does not dry out. During cold weather, however, the ground freezes. The roots cannot get much water. If the leaves kept giving off water, the tree would dry up and die.

In the fall, a layer of cork grows at the bottom of each leaf stem, blocking water from flowing into the leaf. The leaf dries up. It is easily shaken off the tree by the wind, and it falls to the ground.

DID YOU KNOW...?

• The hottest temperature ever recorded was in the country of Libya in North Africa. There, in one place in 1922, the temperature reached more than 136 degrees Fahrenheit! If you look at an air thermometer, you will see that the numbers on it don't even go that high!

• The place with the coldest temperature on record is near the South Pole. At a weather station called Vostok, 400 miles from the Pole, the temperature has gotten colder than 126 degrees below zero Fahrenheit. You'd need warm clothes in weather that cold!

• Some plants eat animals! These plants can make their own food, but they need additional minerals that they cannot get from the soil. They get this extra food from the insects, small birds, or mice that they eat! Three of the animal-eating plants are the pitcher plant, the sundew, and the Venus's-flytrap. The pitcher plant has leaves shaped like pitchers or vases. The bottom of each pitcher contains water. If an insect, bird, or mouse falls inside, it drowns. The sundew has leaves covered with many hairs. At the tip of each hair is a sticky liquid that shines like dew in the sunlight. When an insect lands on a leaf, it gets caught in the sticky drops. The hairs bend over the insect and hold it down as the plant digests it. The Venus's-flytrap has leaves that fold in half and close like a trap. Each leaf has little hairs on it. When an insect lands on the hairs, the two halves of the leaf close, trapping the insect. When the plant has finished eating, the leaf opens up again, to wait for another victim.

I GAVE MY REPORT IN SCHOOL TODAY...

AT THE END I SAID, "THIS REPORT WAS WRITTEN ON RECYCLED PAPER...NO TREES WERE DESTROYED TO MAKE THIS REPORT"

DID THE TEACHER APPRECIATE IT?

NO, BUT THE TREES DID!

● Every day we use things that come from plants. Things made of wood—houses, fences, furniture, and paper—come from the trunks of trees.

Rubber comes from the sap of the rubber tree. Tires, shoe heels, rubber balls, diving suits, and many toys are made of rubber.

Cotton cloth is made from the cotton plant, and linen cloth is made from the flax plant. Clothes, curtains, and sheets are some of the things made from cotton and linen.

Medicines, too, come from plants. Quinine, used to treat malaria, comes from the bark of the cinchona (sin-KOE-nuh) tree. Digitalis (dij-ih-TAL-iss), used to treat weak hearts, is made from the dried leaves of the foxglove plant.

● Old Faithful is a geyser (GUY-zur) in Yellowstone National Park, Wyoming. A geyser is a special kind of hot spring. Its water gets so hot under-ground that it boils and explodes into steam. The geyser shoots the hot water and steam into the air from an opening in the ground. The water shoots up like a foun-tain for a while, and then dies down.

Some geysers spurt only once every few years. Old Faithful got its name by shooting

water faithfully about once every 30 to 80 minutes for more than 100 years. It shoots the water more than 130 feet high!

● Rainbows are made when sunlight shines through moisture in the sky. The tiny drops of water break the light into beautiful colors.

EVEN I LIKE RAINBOWS!

◆ IN THE ◆
NEXT VOLUME

Have you ever wondered where echoes come from, or what makes cartoon characters move, or how scuba divers breathe underwater? You can find answers to these questions and lots more in volume 8, *Science Can Be Super—Sound, Light, and Air.*

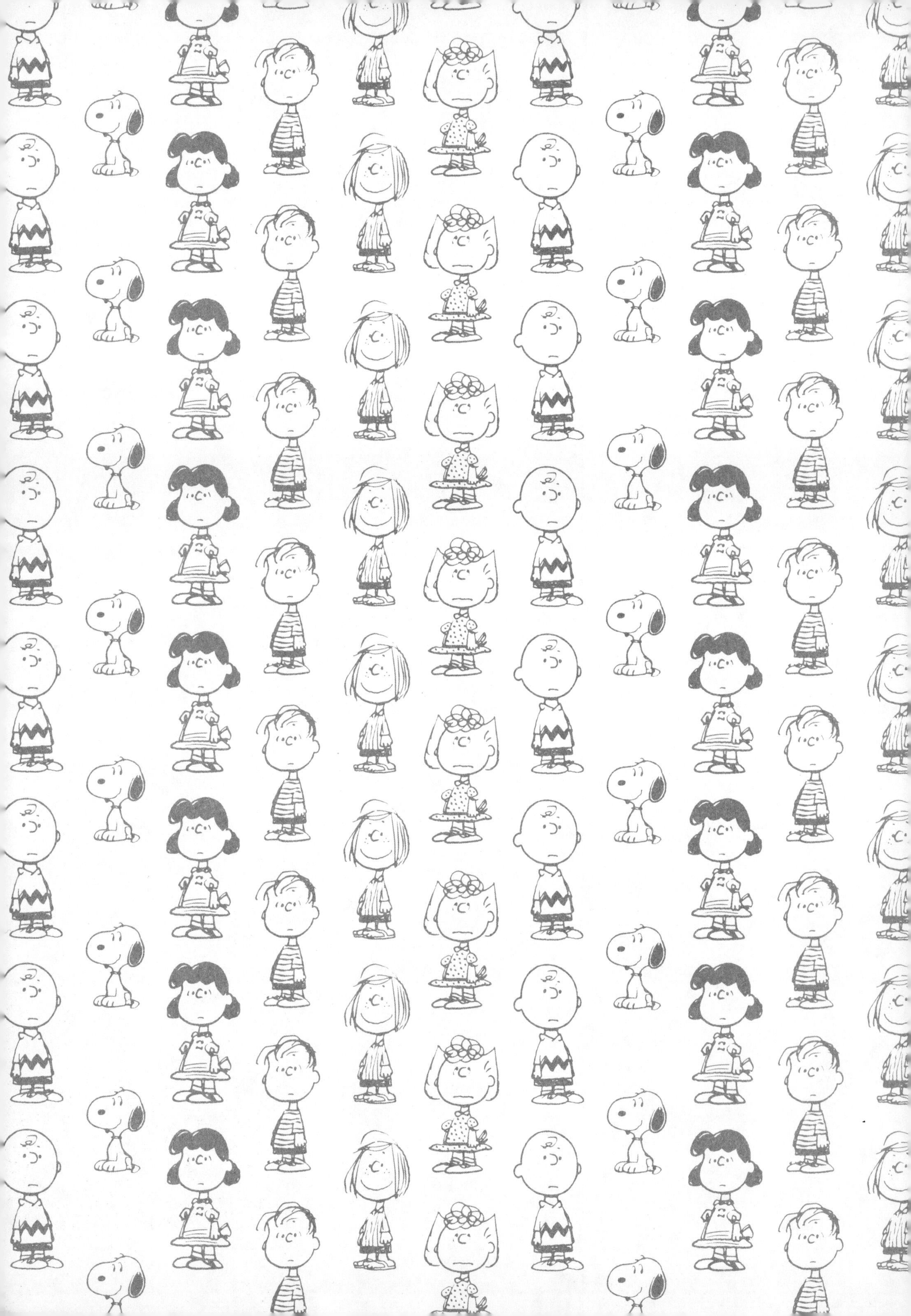